Caleb Has Something to Say

Written by Chanita Stone
Illustrated by
Vladimir Cebu LL.B.

Written by Stone LLC

Dedication

This book is dedicated to my son, Caleb. I want you to know that you belong. There is always space for you in this world. It is not your special needs that make you special. Your greatness was already assigned to you way before there was any thought of a diagnosis. Your light was going to shine bright, differently abled or not. You have a purpose. You have a path that is all yours, and I am grateful to be on this journey with you.

My name is Caleb, and I am five years old.
While I was being born, my brain got hurt
really badly. The doctors told my mom
and dad I would have to live with
something called, Cerebral Palsy.

For me, that means sometimes I will do things differently than other kids around me. One thing that I do differently is how I communicate. I am non-verbal. That means I do not talk.

But just because I do
not speak my words...

Does not mean I don't
have anything to say.

When I am happy, you'll know it. My smile will be so big and wide that you'll see all of my teeth.

Like when my dad comes in from work and says, "Hey, buddy!" as he pats my chest. I get so excited that he is home. It makes me laugh and giggle.

Sometimes I just really need a hug. I might have a tummy ache, or maybe my body has tightened up too much and I can't relax. All of these things can make me feel sad.

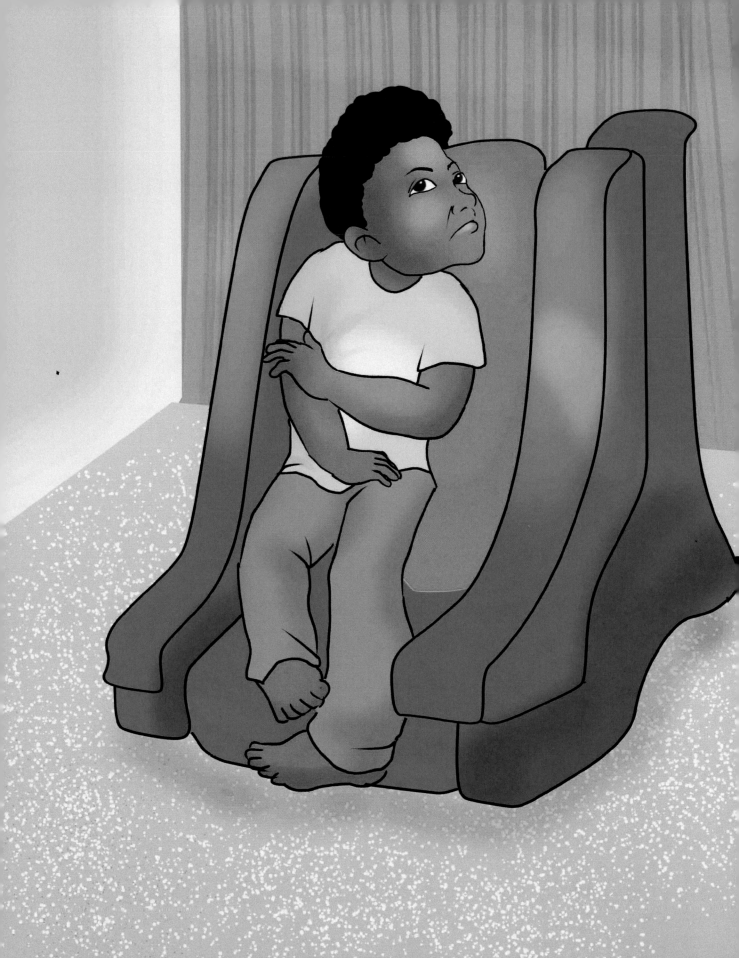

You'll know I'm sad because my shoulders slump and my head hangs low. I'll whimper a little, or maybe even...

"WAAAAAAHHHH!" cry out loud!
And my sister always comes to
comfort me.

When it's time for me to eat, you'll know! I will open and close my mouth, chomping my teeth. I'll smack my lips to say "Hey! I'm ready for something yummy!"

And if it hits the spot, like the cotton candy my TMa gives me, I'll keep turning my head to you, letting you know, "I want more, please!"

Just like you, there are times
that I don't feel like talking
or I just need a break.

When that happens, I may turn
my head away like this...

And if you don't get the picture, then I just close my eyes like this.

People will think I'm sleeping... but not my mom! She says, "Caleb, I know you are awake!" And she's right.

My mom also knows when I am tired. When she picks me up, I melt right into her arms. She kisses my forehead as she rocks me and hums the most beautiful tune.

I start to have big and deep yawns. My eyes begin to blink slower and slower...

And before I know it, I'm having sweet, sweet dreams.

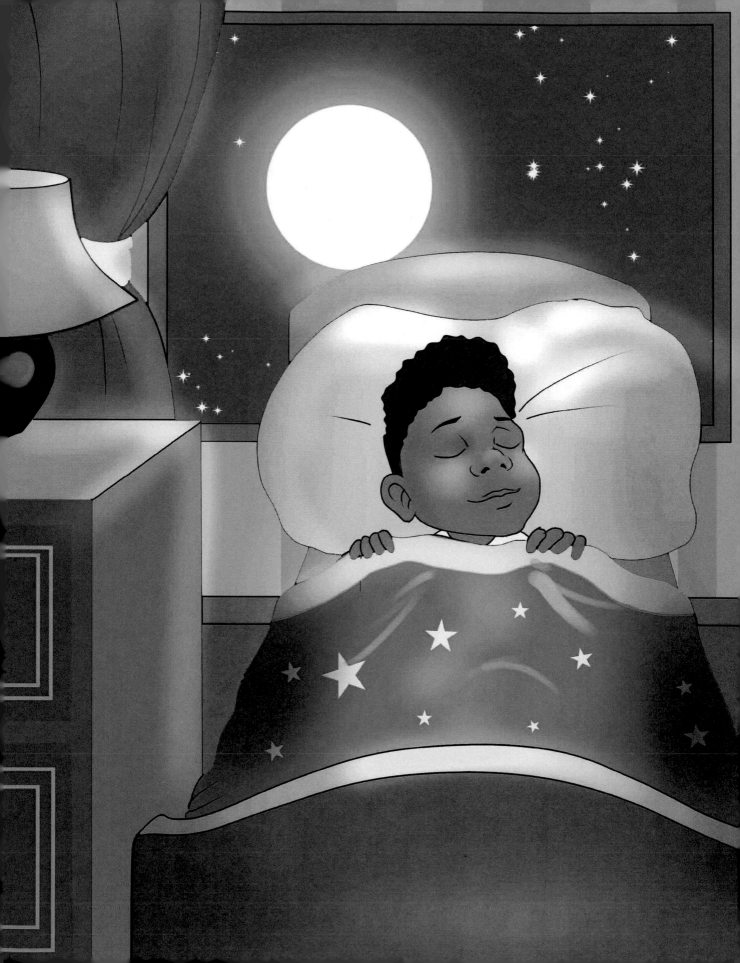

To the parents...

I'm sending you a great big hug and offering these words of encouragement from a place of understanding. You are doing a great job! With every decision you make on behalf of your child, I know you are doing so with their best interest at heart. We have been given a responsibility that is not to be taken lightly. We are our children's advocates for whatever they need or want in this life. The opinions and questions from others may weigh on you...or not! But just know someone understands and is rooting for you and your families, to grow in continued health, happiness, and love.

To the children...

You all are some amazing children. Look at you, inspiring myself, your parents, and everyone who knows you! We all know that you have something to say, and we are eagerly listening, waiting to hear you! Continue to shine your light as bright as you can. You are smart, you are capable, you are loved. And like I tell my little ones, you can do ANYTHING you set your beautiful mind to do.

Made in the USA
Las Vegas, NV
27 July 2021